UNLOCKING THE POWER WITHIN

NIDHI'S JOURNEY TO MASTERING HER MINDSET

NIDHI DOHARE

Made with ❤ on the Notion Press Platform
www.notionpress.com

Contents

Preface

In the vast tapestry of human experience, there are stories that resonate deeply within us, touching our hearts and inspiring us to dream, to believe, and to act. The story you are about to embark on is one such tale—a journey of empowerment, resilience, and hope that spans continents and generations.

At its core, this story is a celebration of the human spirit—the indomitable force that drives us to overcome adversity, to pursue our dreams, and to create a better world for ourselves and others. Through the experiences of its characters, we are invited to explore the transformative power of mindset mastery, the importance of community and collaboration, and the boundless potential that lies within each of us.

As you immerse yourself in the pages that follow, I invite you to reflect on your own journey and the role you play in shaping the world around you. May this story inspire you to embrace your own power, to cultivate resilience in the face of challenges, and to believe in the limitless possibilities that await when we dare to dream.

With an open heart and a sense of wonder, let us embark on this journey together—a journey of discovery, growth, and empowerment that reminds us of the extraordinary capacity we all possess to create positive change in our lives and in the world.

Acknowledgements

I would like to express my deepest gratitude to all those who have contributed to the creation of this story.

First and foremost, I want to thank the individuals and organizations working tirelessly to empower others and create positive change in the world. Your dedication and passion inspire us all to strive for a better future.

To my Parents, mentors, colleagues, and friends who have supported and encouraged me throughout this journey, thank you for your invaluable guidance and insight. Your wisdom has been instrumental in shaping the narrative of this story.

A special thank you to the readers who have joined me on this adventure. Your engagement and enthusiasm have fueled my creativity and inspired me to delve deeper into the themes of empowerment, resilience, and hope.

Together, we can continue to create stories that uplift, inspire, and empower others to make a difference in the world.

With heartfelt thanks,
Nidhi Dohare

CHAPTER ONE

The Breaking Point

Nidhi sat in her spacious corner office, the afternoon sunlight filtering through the floor-to-ceiling windows. The sleek, modern furnishings and the stunning view of the city skyline usually filled her with a sense of pride and accomplishment. But today, as she stared down at the performance review in her hands, a heavy weight settled in the pit of her stomach.

Despite her impressive track record, her ambitious goals, and her unwavering work ethic, Nidhi couldn't shake the nagging feeling that she was never quite good enough. The feedback from her superiors, while constructive, had once again highlighted the areas where she fell short. The words "lacks confidence" and "hesitant to take risks" jumped out at her, cutting deeper than she cared to admit.

Nidhi leaned back in her chair, her brow furrowed in frustration. She had climbed the corporate ladder with determination, driven by a relentless pursuit of success. Yet, no matter how many accolades she earned or milestones she achieved, she couldn't silence the inner critic that constantly undermined her confidence.

As she re-read the review, Nidhi felt a familiar sense of self-doubt creeping in. She had always been her own harshest critic, second-guessing every decision, every presentation, every interaction with her colleagues. The fear of failure had become a constant companion, holding her back from reaching her full potential.

Nidhi closed her eyes, taking a deep, steadying breath. She had to face the truth – her limiting beliefs and self-doubt had become the greatest obstacles in her path to success. Frustrated and dejected, she realized that she could no longer ignore the need to address the root causes of this debilitating mindset.

With a renewed sense of determination, Nidhi made a bold decision. She would seek out the guidance of Aisha, a renowned life coach and mindset expert, to unlock the secrets to mastering her mindset and unleashing her true power. It was time to confront her fears head-on and embark on a transformative journey of self-discovery., Nidhi's gaze drifted back to the performance review, the words blurring as she fought back the sting of tears. She had always prided herself on her resilience, her ability to push through challenges and excel, but this time, the feedback felt like a gut punch.

Slowly, the realization dawned on her – her limiting beliefs and inner critic had been the true obstacles standing in her way, not the external pressures or expectations of her superiors. All this time, she had been her own worst enemy, undermining her confidence and holding herself back from reaching her full potential.

Nidhi let out a frustrated sigh, her fingers tightening around the edges of the document. How many opportunities had she missed, how many bold moves had she shied away from, all because she had been too consumed by self-doubt and insecurity? The thought was both infuriating and humbling.

Leaning forward, Nidhi rested her elbows on the desk, burying her face in her hands. She had to face the truth – she could no longer ignore the root causes of her self-doubt. If she wanted to break free from this cycle of self-sabotage, she would need to confront her fears and limiting beliefs head-on.

The path forward would not be easy, Nidhi knew that much. But the alternative – continuing to let her inner critic hold her back – was simply unacceptable. With a renewed sense of determination, she lifted her head, her eyes narrowing with resolve. It was time to take control of her mindset and unlock the power that lay dormant within her. Nidhi knew what she had to do. With a deep breath, she reached for her phone and scrolled through her contacts, finally landing on the name she had been considering for weeks – Aisha, a renowned life coach and mindset expert.

As Nidhi pressed the call button, a sense of both trepidation and hope swirled within her. This was a pivotal moment, a crossroads where she could either continue down the path of self-doubt or take a bold leap towards transformation.

The line clicked, and Aisha's warm, reassuring voice filled Nidhi's ears. "Hello, Nidhi. I'm so glad you reached out. How can I help you today?"

Nidhi hesitated for a moment, her heart pounding in her chest. But then the words came tumbling out, a torrent of frustration, self-criticism, and a deep, underlying desire for change.

Aisha listened intently, her gaze unwavering and her expression one of empathy and understanding. When Nidhi finally fell silent, Aisha spoke, her voice soothing and insightful.

"Nidhi, I can hear the weight of your struggles, but I also sense the determination that burns within you. This is a pivotal moment – a chance for you to unlock the true power that lies dormant, waiting to be unleashed."

Nidhi felt a glimmer of hope ignite within her as Aisha continued, outlining the transformative journey that lay ahead. The life coach spoke of mindset mastery, of confronting fears and shattering limiting beliefs, and of the profound personal growth that could come from such a journey.

With each word, Nidhi felt a shift within her, a stirring of possibilities that she had long ago resigned herself to. The path ahead would not be easy, but the prospect of finally breaking free from the shackles of self-doubt filled her with a sense of determination she hadn't felt in years.

"I'm ready," Nidhi said, her voice steady and resolute. "I'm ready to do whatever it takes to master my mindset and unlock my true potential."

Aisha smiled, a knowing gleam in her eyes. "Then let's begin." Aisha leaned forward, her gaze steady and her tone measured as she introduced Nidhi to the core principles of mindset mastery.

"The key to unlocking your true potential, Nidhi, lies not in your external circumstances, but in the way you perceive and interact with the world around you," Aisha explained. "Our beliefs, thoughts, and perceptions shape our reality, determining the limits of what we believe ourselves capable of achieving."

Nidhi listened intently, her brow furrowed in concentration as Aisha's words sank in. It was a revelation, a stark contrast to the narrative she had been telling herself for years – that her self-doubt and insecurities were simply inherent flaws that she had to learn to manage.

"The process of mindset mastery," Aisha continued, "requires us to confront those limiting beliefs head-on, to challenge the negative narratives that have been holding us back. It's not an easy journey, but I can assure you, the rewards are profound."

Nidhi felt a flutter of trepidation in the pit of her stomach. The prospect of delving into the depths of her own psyche, of unearthing the root causes of her self-doubt, was both daunting and intriguing.

As if sensing her hesitation, Aisha reached across the desk and placed a reassuring hand on Nidhi's arm. "I know it can be scary, Nidhi. But I believe in you, and I know that you have the strength and resilience to overcome these obstacles. This journey will test you, but it will also transform you in ways you can't yet imagine."

Nidhi felt a surge of determination rise within her, pushing back against the fear that had so often held her captive. If Aisha believed in her, then perhaps she could learn to believe in herself as well. With a resolute nod, she steeled herself for the challenges that lay ahead.

"I'm ready," Nidhi said, her voice steady. "Let's do this.", As Aisha delved deeper into the various mindset-shifting techniques and strategies, Nidhi found herself leaning forward, her initial skepticism gradually giving way to a glimmer of hope.

Affirmations, visualization, and mindfulness practices – Aisha outlined a comprehensive toolkit that Nidhi could use to rewire her subconscious mind and break free from the shackles of self-doubt.

The life coach spoke with unwavering conviction, her words painting a vivid picture of the transformative journey that lay ahead. Nidhi listened, captivated, as Aisha described how these practices could help her reframe her perspective, cultivate a more positive and empowering mindset, and unlock her true potential.

Nidhi couldn't help but feel a stirring of excitement within her. For so long, she had resigned herself to the limitations of her self-doubt, convinced that it was an inherent part of who she was. But now, as Aisha outlined a path towards mastering her mindset, Nidhi recognized the profound potential for personal growth and transformation.

This won't be easy, Aisha cautioned, her gaze meeting Nidhi's with sincerity. Confronting your fears and shattering your limiting beliefs will require courage, resilience, and a deep commitment to the process. But I believe in you, Nidhi. I've seen what's possible when someone is willing to do the work.

Nidhi felt a surge of determination coursing through her veins. She had spent far too long allowing her self-doubt to hold her back, to dictate the limits of her ambitions and dreams. Now, with Aisha's guidance and the promise of a transformative journey ahead, Nidhi was ready to take the leap.

I'm in, she said, her voice firm and resolute. I'm ready to do whatever it takes to unlock the power that's been dormant inside me. Let's get started.

Aisha's lips curled into a warm, encouraging smile. Then let the journey begin. As Nidhi prepared for her first intensive workshop with Aisha, a sense of anticipation and trepidation swirled within her. This was a pivotal moment, a crossroads where she could either continue down the path of self-doubt and limitation or embark on a transformative journey of self-discovery.

Nidhi couldn't help but reflect on the events that had led her to this point – the disheartening performance review, the crushing realization that her own limiting beliefs had been her greatest obstacle, and the bold decision to seek out Aisha's guidance. It had been a humbling and eye- opening experience, forcing her to confront the harsh truths she had long tried to ignore.

A part of her still harbored a deep-seated fear of the unknown, of the challenges and emotional upheaval that lay ahead. What if she couldn't overcome her self-doubt? What if she failed, despite her best efforts? The questions swirled in her mind, a familiar chorus of self-criticism and uncertainty.

But beneath the trepidation, Nidhi could feel a spark of determination igniting within her. She had spent far too long allowing her insecurities to dictate the course of her life, to hold her back from reaching her full potential. Now, with Aisha's guidance and the promise of a transformative journey, Nidhi was ready to confront those obstacles head-on.

Taking a deep, steadying breath, Nidhi steeled herself for the challenges that lay ahead. The path would not be easy, but she was no longer willing to settle for anything less than the limitless possibilities that awaited her. With a renewed sense of purpose, she stepped into the unknown, ready to unlock the power that had been dormant within her for far too long.

CHAPTER TWO

The Awakening

Nidhi stood at the entrance of Aisha's serene studio, a modern sanctuary nestled in the heart of the bustling city. The calming ambiance, with its soft lighting and minimalist décor, immediately eased some of her anxiety. She took a deep breath and stepped inside, feeling the weight of her decision settling into a sense of anticipation.

Aisha greeted her with a warm smile and led her to a comfortable seating area. "Welcome, Nidhi. I'm glad you're here," she said, her voice soothing and reassuring.

Nidhi nodded, her apprehension mingling with a burgeoning sense of hope. "Thank you, Aisha. I'm ready to begin."

Aisha settled into a chair across from Nidhi and began to outline the structure of their sessions. "Our work together will be a combination of introspection, practical exercises, and developing new habits to reframe your mindset. We'll start by exploring your core beliefs and the stories you've been telling yourself."

Nidhi listened intently, feeling a mix of curiosity and apprehension. The idea of delving into the depths of her psyche was daunting, but she knew it was necessary for her growth.

"Let's start with a simple exercise," Aisha suggested. "Close your eyes and take a few deep breaths. Focus on the rise and fall of your chest, letting go of any tension."

Nidhi followed Aisha's instructions, feeling the tension gradually melt away as she centered herself in the present moment.

"Now," Aisha continued, "I want you to think about a recent situation where you felt overwhelmed by self-doubt. Visualize it clearly in your mind."

Nidhi's thoughts drifted to a recent presentation at work, where she had stumbled over her words and felt a wave of anxiety wash over her. The memory was vivid, the sting of embarrassment still fresh.

"Can you describe what you felt and thought in that moment?" Aisha asked gently.

Nidhi hesitated, then spoke softly. "I felt exposed, like everyone could see my incompetence. I thought I was a fraud, that I didn't belong there."

Aisha nodded, her expression compassionate. "Thank you for sharing that, Nidhi. These thoughts and feelings are part of the narrative you've been carrying with you. Now, let's challenge them."

Nidhi opened her eyes, meeting Aisha's steady gaze. "How?" she asked, a note of determination in her voice.

"We'll start by questioning the validity of these thoughts," Aisha explained. "Ask yourself: Is it absolutely true that you're incompetent? Are there instances where you've been successful and confident?"

Nidhi considered this, recalling moments when she had excelled in her career, received praise, and felt genuinely proud of her achievements. "No, it's not absolutely true," she admitted. "There have been times when I've been successful."

Aisha smiled encouragingly. "Exactly. Our goal is to shift your focus from these negative narratives to a more balanced perspective. Recognize your successes and allow them to counteract the self-doubt."

As the session progressed, Aisha guided Nidhi through various exercises to identify and challenge her limiting beliefs. They explored the origins of these beliefs, tracing them back to past experiences and societal influences.

Nidhi found herself uncovering deeply ingrained patterns of thought that had shaped her self-perception for years. It was a challenging process, filled with moments of vulnerability and self-discovery. Yet, with each revelation, she felt a gradual lightening of the burden she had carried for so long.

By the end of the session, Nidhi felt a sense of clarity and empowerment. Aisha's guidance had illuminated a path forward, one that required dedication and resilience but promised profound transformation.

A few days later, Nidhi sat in her living room, surrounded by the quiet hum of the city outside. She was engrossed in the journal Aisha had encouraged her to keep, capturing her thoughts, fears, and reflections. It was an exercise in vulnerability, but one that was proving to be deeply cathartic.

The phone rang, jolting her from her introspection. It was Aisha, calling for their scheduled check-in. Nidhi answered, feeling a mix of anticipation and readiness.

"Hi, Aisha," she greeted, her voice steady.

"Hi, Nidhi. How are you feeling today?" Aisha asked, her tone warm and encouraging.

"I‘m doing well," Nidhi replied. "I’ve been journaling as you suggested, and it’s been... eye-opening."

"I’m glad to hear that," Aisha said. "Journaling is a powerful tool for self-awareness. Have you noticed any recurring themes or patterns in your thoughts?"

Nidhi paused, reflecting on the past few entries. "Yes, actually. I realize that a lot of my self-doubt stems from a fear of judgment and failure. I keep replaying moments where I felt inadequate, and it reinforces this belief that I'm not good enough."

"That’s a crucial insight, Nidhi," Aisha affirmed. "The next step is to challenge those beliefs and reframe those experiences. Remember, failure is not a reflection of your worth but an opportunity for growth."

Nidhi nodded, absorbing Aisha's words. "It makes sense, but it's hard to let go of that fear."

"It is," Aisha agreed. "But each time you confront and reframe these thoughts, you're weakening their hold on you. It takes practice and persistence."

They continued to discuss strategies for reframing negative thoughts, and Aisha introduced Nidhi to the concept of affirmations – positive statements that could help rewire her subconscious mind. They worked together to create a list of personalized affirmations that resonated with Nidhi's aspirations and values.

Over the next few weeks, Nidhi immersed herself in the practices Aisha had taught her. She started each day with affirmations, visualizing her goals and successes with a sense of conviction she hadn't felt in years. She practiced mindfulness, grounding herself in the present and quieting the incessant chatter of her inner critic.

The changes were subtle at first – a newfound confidence in meetings, a willingness to speak up and share her ideas, a gradual easing of the self-doubt that had once dominated her thoughts. She began to notice her achievements more, allowing herself to feel proud and capable.

One evening, after a particularly successful presentation, Nidhi sat in her office, the city lights twinkling outside. She pulled out her journal and began to write, capturing the sense of accomplishment and the positive feedback she had received.

As she wrote, a realization struck her – she was beginning to believe in herself. The inner critic that had once been so loud was now a faint whisper, easily drowned out by her growing self-assurance.

The journey was far from over, but Nidhi could see the path ahead with clarity and purpose. She was no longer a prisoner of her self-doubt but a warrior, forging her own destiny with each step she took.

Closing her journal, Nidhi leaned back in her chair, a smile playing on her lips. For the first time in a long while, she felt truly alive, ready to embrace the limitless possibilities that lay ahead.

CHAPTER THREE

Confronting Shadows

Nidhi's progress was palpable, yet the journey was just beginning. As the weeks turned into months, she diligently practiced the techniques Aisha had taught her. Her confidence grew, and the inner critic that once dictated her life began to fade. But Nidhi knew that true transformation required confronting the deeper shadows lurking in her past.

One breezy Saturday afternoon, Nidhi arrived at Aisha's studio for an intensive session. This time, she felt a mixture of resolve and trepidation. Today, they were going to dive into her past experiences, unearthing the roots of her self-doubt.

Aisha welcomed her with the usual warmth. "Good to see you, Nidhi. Are you ready for today's session?"

Nidhi took a deep breath and nodded. "Yes, I am."

They settled into the comfortable seating area, the soft glow of the afternoon sun casting a peaceful light over the room. Aisha began with a grounding exercise, guiding Nidhi to focus on her breath and center herself in the present moment.

"We're going to explore some of the formative experiences that have shaped your self-beliefs," Aisha explained. "This process can be challenging, but it's essential for healing and growth."

Nidhi nodded, feeling a knot of anticipation in her stomach. She closed her eyes as Aisha guided her into a deep state of relaxation, her voice soothing and steady.

"Think back to a time in your life when you first felt the sting of self-doubt," Aisha instructed. "Allow the memory to come to you, and when it does, describe it to me."

Nidhi's mind drifted back to her teenage years, a period marked by academic pressure and the constant need to prove herself. A particular memory surfaced – a high school debate competition where she had frozen on stage, unable to articulate her arguments. The disappointment in her teachers' eyes, the whispers of her classmates, and the sense of failure that had enveloped her.

"I remember a debate competition in high school," Nidhi began, her voice trembling slightly. "I was so nervous. I couldn't get my words out. I felt like I had let everyone down – my teachers, my team, myself."

Aisha listened intently, her expression one of empathy and understanding. "Thank you for sharing that, Nidhi. It's clear that this experience left a deep impact on you. Let's explore how it shaped your self-beliefs."

As they delved into the memory, Nidhi realized how that moment had planted the seeds of her self-doubt. The fear of judgment, the pressure to excel, and the harsh self-criticism had taken root, influencing her actions and decisions for years to come.

"That experience made me feel like a failure," Nidhi admitted. "And every time I faced a challenge, that fear of failure resurfaced."

Aisha nodded. "It's important to recognize how these past experiences influence our present. But it's also crucial to reframe them and release their hold on us."

They worked through the memory, challenging the narrative that had been built around it. Aisha guided Nidhi to see the courage it took to participate in the competition, the valuable lessons learned, and the growth that came from it.

"You were brave to stand up there," Aisha pointed out. "And even though it didn't go as planned, it was a step towards becoming the person you are today."

Nidhi felt a shift within her, a loosening of the grip that memory had held over her for so long. They continued to explore other significant moments from her past, reframing each one with compassion and understanding.

By the end of the session, Nidhi felt a profound sense of release. It was as if a weight she had carried for years had finally been lifted. She looked at Aisha, her eyes filled with gratitude.

"Thank you, Aisha," she said softly. "I feel... lighter."

Aisha smiled warmly. "You're doing incredible work, Nidhi. Remember, this is a journey. Be patient with yourself and celebrate every step forward."

Nidhi left the studio that day with a renewed sense of purpose. She understood now that her self-doubt was not an inherent flaw but a collection of stories she had been telling herself. And with each session, she was rewriting those stories, reclaiming her narrative.

Back at home, Nidhi continued her practices with even greater dedication. She meditated, journaled, and repeated her affirmations daily. She also started to seek out new challenges, embracing opportunities that once intimidated her.

One evening, as she sat reflecting on her journey, a notification popped up on her phone – an invitation to speak at a women's leadership conference. The old Nidhi would have hesitated, plagued by self-doubt and fear of failure. But the new Nidhi felt a spark of excitement.

She accepted the invitation with a sense of confidence she hadn't felt in years. This was her chance to not only share her story but to inspire others facing similar struggles. It was a culmination of the work she had been doing, a testament to her transformation.

The day of the conference arrived, and Nidhi stood backstage, ready to step into the spotlight. She took a deep breath, recalling the techniques Aisha had taught her. She felt the familiar flutter of nerves but this time, it was accompanied by a deep sense of calm and assurance.

As she walked onto the stage, the audience's applause filled the room. Nidhi stood tall, her gaze sweeping over the sea of faces. She began her speech, sharing her journey of overcoming self-doubt and embracing her true potential.

The words flowed effortlessly, her voice steady and confident. She spoke of the challenges, the breakthroughs, and the invaluable lessons learned. She saw nods of understanding, tears of empathy, and smiles of encouragement.

When she finished, the applause was thunderous. Nidhi felt a surge of pride and fulfillment. She had not only conquered her fears but had also touched the lives of others.

As she stepped off the stage, she spotted Aisha in the audience, beaming with pride. Nidhi walked over and hugged her tightly. "Thank you, Aisha. I couldn't have done this without you."

Aisha smiled, her eyes twinkling. "You did this, Nidhi. You unlocked the power within you. I'm so proud of you."

Nidhi realized that this was just the beginning. The journey of self-discovery and growth was ongoing, filled with endless possibilities. And with each step forward, she was becoming the person she was always meant to be – confident, resilient, and truly empowered.

CHAPTER FOUR

Embracing Change

Nidhi's success at the women's leadership conference was a turning point. She returned to work with a renewed sense of purpose and a confidence that resonated with her colleagues. Her boss noticed the change almost immediately.

"Nidhi, I've seen a new spark in you lately," her boss remarked during a meeting. "Your presentation at the conference was outstanding. I'd like you to lead the new project we've been planning."

The new project was a significant opportunity, one that involved coordinating with international teams and presenting strategies to the board of directors. A few months ago, Nidhi might have hesitated, but now, she accepted the challenge with enthusiasm.

"Thank you. I'm looking forward to it," she replied, her voice steady and assured.

Over the next few weeks, Nidhi immersed herself in the project. She led with confidence, navigating complex problems with a calm demeanor and inspiring her team with her positive energy. Her growth mindset became contagious, fostering a collaborative and innovative atmosphere.

One afternoon, as she prepared for a critical presentation to the board, her phone buzzed. It was a message from Aisha.

"Thinking of you today. Remember, you've got this!"

Nidhi smiled, feeling a wave of gratitude. She had come so far, and Aisha's support had been instrumental. She took a deep breath, centered herself, and walked into the boardroom.

The presentation went exceptionally well. The board members were impressed with her strategic insights and clear vision. As they applauded, Nidhi felt a deep sense of accomplishment. She had not only faced her fears but had also thrived under pressure.

After the meeting, Nidhi found a quiet moment to reflect in her office. She thought about her journey – the performance review that had triggered her self-doubt, the sessions with Aisha, the transformation she had undergone. She realized that her growth was not just about professional success but also about personal fulfillment and inner peace.

Her thoughts were interrupted by a knock on the door. It was Priya, a junior colleague who had recently joined the team.

"Hi, Nidhi. Can I talk to you for a minute?" Priya asked, her voice tentative.

"Of course, Priya. Come in," Nidhi replied warmly.

Priya sat down, looking nervous. "I just wanted to say that your leadership and the way you handled the project have been really inspiring. I've been struggling with confidence myself, and seeing you succeed has given me hope."

Nidhi felt a surge of empathy. She saw a reflection of her younger self in Priya's eyes. "Thank you, Priya. I understand how you feel. I've been there too. If you'd like, I can share some of the strategies that helped me."

Priya's eyes lit up. "I would love that. Thank you so much, Nidhi."

In the following weeks, Nidhi took Priya under her wing, mentoring her and sharing the mindset techniques she had learned from Aisha. She encouraged Priya to embrace challenges, celebrate small victories, and silence her inner critic.

Watching Priya's confidence grow reminded Nidhi of her own journey. It was rewarding to see how her transformation was positively impacting others. She realized that her story could inspire many more, and she decided to expand her efforts beyond the office.

Nidhi approached the HR department with an idea – to start a mentorship and personal development program within the company. The program would focus on mindset mastery, resilience, and leadership skills, empowering employees to reach their full potential.

The HR team embraced the idea, and soon, Nidhi found herself leading workshops and coaching sessions, sharing her experiences and insights. The program quickly gained popularity, with employees reporting increased confidence and motivation.

Outside of work, Nidhi continued to deepen her personal growth. She maintained her daily practices of journaling, meditation, and affirmations. She also pursued new interests, such as yoga and creative writing, which brought her joy and balance.

Her relationship with Aisha evolved into a close friendship. They often met for coffee, discussing their journeys and aspirations. Aisha continued to provide guidance, but now, their conversations were more about celebrating progress and exploring new possibilities.

One evening, as Nidhi sat on her balcony, watching the city lights twinkle, she felt a profound sense of contentment. She had transformed her life in ways she had once thought impossible. Her journey was far from over, but she was ready for whatever came next.

Her phone buzzed with a new message – an invitation to speak at a national leadership summit. Nidhi smiled, feeling a familiar excitement. She accepted the invitation, knowing that this was another opportunity to share her story and inspire others.

On the day of the summit, Nidhi stood backstage, her heart pounding with anticipation. She thought about the path that had led her here – the challenges, the growth, the unwavering support of Aisha. She felt a deep sense of gratitude and pride.

As she stepped onto the stage, the audience's applause echoed in her ears. Nidhi stood tall, her gaze sweeping over the sea of faces. She began her speech, sharing her journey of overcoming self-doubt and embracing change.

The words flowed effortlessly, her voice strong and confident. She spoke of the power of mindset, the importance of resilience, and the beauty of self-discovery. She saw nods of understanding, tears of empathy, and smiles of encouragement.

When she finished, the applause was thunderous. Nidhi felt a surge of pride and fulfillment. She had not only conquered her fears but had also touched the lives of others.

As she stepped off the stage, she spotted Aisha in the audience, beaming with pride. Nidhi walked over and hugged her tightly.

"Thank you, Aisha. I couldn't have done this without you."

Aisha smiled, her eyes twinkling. "You did this, Nidhi. You unlocked the power within you. I'm so proud of you."

Nidhi realized that this was just the beginning. The journey of self-discovery and growth was ongoing, filled with endless possibilities. And with each step forward, she was becoming the person she was always meant to be – confident, resilient, and truly empowered.

CHAPTER FIVE

Building Bridges

Nidhi's speech at the national leadership summit had been a resounding success. She received numerous invitations to speak at other events and workshops, and her inbox was flooded with messages from people inspired by her story. Nidhi embraced these opportunities, seeing them as a way to extend her influence and help others unlock their potential.

One morning, as she was reviewing her schedule, a message caught her eye. It was from Dr. Rajiv Patel, a renowned psychologist and author who had written extensively on leadership and personal growth.

"Dear Nidhi,

I attended your talk at the summit and was profoundly moved by your story and insights. I believe we share a common vision of empowering individuals to overcome their inner barriers. I would love to collaborate on a project that can reach even more people. If you're interested, let's discuss this further.

Best regards, Dr. Rajiv Patel"

Nidhi's heart raced with excitement. A collaboration with Dr. Patel was a remarkable opportunity. She quickly replied, expressing her enthusiasm and setting up a meeting.

A few days later, Nidhi met Dr. Patel at a cozy café downtown. He was a tall man with a kind face and a calm, thoughtful demeanor. They exchanged pleasantries before diving into the discussion.

"Nidhi, your journey is incredibly inspiring," Dr. Patel began. "I've been working on a new book about overcoming self-doubt, and I think your story and insights would add tremendous value. I'd like you to co-author this book with me."

Nidhi was taken aback. Writing a book was a significant commitment, but the prospect of reaching a wider audience and sharing her experiences on a larger platform was exhilarating.

"I would be honored, Dr. Patel," she replied, her voice filled with excitement. "I believe we can make a real impact together."

They spent the next few hours brainstorming ideas and outlining the book. It would combine personal anecdotes, practical strategies, and psychological insights to provide a comprehensive guide for anyone struggling with self-doubt.

Over the next several months, Nidhi and Dr. Patel worked tirelessly on the book. They met regularly, exchanged drafts, and provided feedback to each other. The process was intense but deeply fulfilling. Nidhi found herself reflecting on her journey, digging deeper into her experiences and the lessons she had learned.

As they neared the completion of the manuscript, Dr. Patel suggested including interviews with other individuals who had overcome significant challenges. Nidhi loved the idea and reached out to several people she had met through her speaking engagements.

One of them was Rani, a young woman who had faced immense adversity in her career and personal life but had emerged stronger and more resilient. Rani's story of perseverance and growth resonated deeply with Nidhi, and she knew it would inspire readers.

The book, titled "Breaking Barriers: A Journey to Overcome Self-Doubt and Unlock Potential," was published to widespread acclaim. Readers praised its authenticity, practical advice, and the diverse stories it featured. Nidhi and Dr. Patel were invited to various talk shows and podcasts, further expanding their reach.

Nidhi's life had taken on a new rhythm. She balanced her corporate responsibilities, speaking engagements, and book promotions with grace and enthusiasm. She continued to mentor Priya and other colleagues, fostering a culture of growth and support within the company.

One evening, after a particularly busy day, Nidhi sat on her balcony, reflecting on her journey. She felt a deep sense of gratitude for the opportunities and challenges that had shaped her path. She thought about Aisha and the profound impact she had on her life.

Impulsively, Nidhi picked up her phone and called Aisha.

"Aisha, I just wanted to thank you again," Nidhi said. "None of this would have been possible without your guidance and support."

Aisha's voice was warm and reassuring. "Nidhi, you've done the work.

I'm incredibly proud of you. Remember, this journey is ongoing. Keep embracing every opportunity for growth and continue to inspire others."

Nidhi's journey continued to evolve. She was invited to join the board of a non-profit organization dedicated to empowering women in the workplace. The organization focused on providing mentorship, resources, and training to help women advance in their careers.

Nidhi accepted the role with enthusiasm, seeing it as another avenue to make a difference. She collaborated with other board members to develop new programs and initiatives, leveraging her experiences and insights to create impactful solutions.

One of the initiatives was a leadership development program for young women from underserved communities. Nidhi poured her heart into the program, designing workshops, and mentoring sessions that would equip participants with the skills and confidence they needed to succeed.

At the inaugural session of the leadership development program, Nidhi stood before a group of eager young women. She shared her story once more, emphasizing the importance of resilience, self-belief, and the willingness to seek help when needed.

"You have the power to shape your destiny," Nidhi said, her voice filled with conviction. "Believe in yourself, embrace challenges, and never let self-doubt hold you back. You are capable of achieving great things."

As she looked into the eyes of her audience, she saw the same spark of determination and hope that had ignited within her. Nidhi knew that her journey had come full circle. She had transformed her life and was now helping others do the same.

Nidhi's impact continued to grow, touching lives and inspiring change. Her story became a beacon of hope for those struggling with self-doubt and insecurity. She had not only unlocked her true potential but had also built bridges for others to cross into their own greatness.

Her journey was far from over, but Nidhi embraced each step with confidence and grace, knowing that the power to overcome and thrive lay within her and within everyone she encountered.

CHAPTER SIX

The Ripple Effect

Months after the successful launch of the leadership development program, Nidhi found herself inundated with emails and messages from participants who had been profoundly impacted by her mentorship. Their stories of personal growth and newfound confidence filled her with a sense of fulfillment she had never experienced before. She realized that the ripple effect of her journey was reaching far beyond what she had initially imagined.

One evening, as she was reviewing testimonials from the program's graduates, her phone rang. It was Dr. Patel.

"Nidhi, I've just received an invitation to speak at the Global Leadership Summit in London," he said, excitement evident in his voice. "They want us to present on our book and discuss the impact of mindset mastery on leadership. Are you interested?"

Nidhi's heart leaped at the opportunity. The Global Leadership Summit was a prestigious event, attracting leaders and influencers from around the world. She knew this was a chance to extend their message on a global scale.

"Absolutely, Dr. Patel. Count me in," she replied, her excitement matching his.

In the weeks leading up to the summit, Nidhi and Dr. Patel meticulously prepared their presentation. They crafted a compelling narrative that intertwined their personal journeys with the practical strategies outlined in their book. Nidhi also reached out to several program graduates to gather their stories, which she planned to share as real-world examples of the principles they advocated.

When the day of the summit arrived, Nidhi felt a mix of nerves and exhilaration. The grandeur of the event was awe-inspiring, with luminaries from various fields congregating to share ideas and insights. As she and Dr. Patel took the stage, Nidhi took a deep breath, centering herself just as Aisha had taught her.

"Good morning, everyone," Dr. Patel began. "Today, we want to take you on a journey of transformation – a journey that begins with overcoming self-doubt and unlocking the limitless potential within each of us."

Nidhi followed, sharing her story with heartfelt authenticity. She spoke of her struggles, the turning points, and the powerful impact of mindset mastery. The audience was captivated, hanging on to every word.

"As we've learned," Nidhi concluded, "the barriers we face are often self-imposed. By changing our mindset, we can transcend these barriers and achieve greatness. This isn't just theory – it's a reality that we've seen time and again."

The presentation was a resounding success. Attendees approached them afterward, expressing gratitude and admiration. Many were eager to implement the strategies in their own lives and organizations.

Back in her hotel room that evening, Nidhi received an unexpected video call from Aisha.

"Nidhi, I just watched your presentation online," Aisha said, her eyes shining with pride. "You were incredible. You've come so far, and your impact is growing every day."

Nidhi felt a swell of emotion. "Thank you, Aisha. Your guidance has been instrumental. I couldn't have done this without you."

The Global Leadership Summit marked a new chapter in Nidhi's journey. Her work gained international recognition, leading to collaborations with organizations worldwide. She and Dr. Patel were invited to co-author another book, this time focusing on case studies of successful leaders who had embraced mindset mastery.

Nidhi also expanded the mentorship and personal development program within her company, adapting it for other branches globally. She traveled frequently, leading workshops and speaking at conferences, always driven by the desire to empower others to overcome their limitations.

One of her most rewarding experiences came from visiting a remote village in India, where she launched an initiative to support young women in education and career development. The program provided scholarships, mentorship, and resources, giving these women opportunities they had never dreamed possible.

During one of these visits, a young girl named Meera approached Nidhi. With tears in her eyes, she said, "Because of you, I believe I can achieve my dreams. Thank you for giving us hope."

Nidhi hugged her, feeling a profound connection. "Meera, you have the power within you. Believe in yourself, and you can accomplish anything."

As Nidhi's influence grew, so did her understanding of the importance of giving back. She established a foundation dedicated to mindset mastery and personal development, focusing on underprivileged communities around the world. The foundation provided resources, training, and support, helping individuals break free from the cycle of self-doubt and achieve their full potential.

Through it all, Nidhi remained grounded in her own practices of self-care and personal growth. She continued to seek Aisha's counsel, valuing her wisdom and friendship. She also nurtured her relationships with family and friends, finding balance amidst her busy life.

One evening, as Nidhi stood on her balcony, she reflected on the incredible journey she had undertaken. From the depths of self-doubt to the heights of global recognition, she had transformed not only her own life but the lives of countless others.

Her phone buzzed with a message from Aisha. "Proud of you, Nidhi. Your journey is an inspiration."

Nidhi smiled, a sense of peace and fulfillment washing over her. She had embraced change, overcome her inner barriers, and discovered the limitless power within her. And now, she was dedicated to helping others do the same.

As she looked out at the city lights, Nidhi knew that her journey was far from over. There were still many more bridges to build, many more lives to touch. And she was ready for whatever the future held, confident in her ability to create positive change, one step at a time.

CHAPTER SEVEN

The Power of Community

Nidhi's foundation, aptly named "Empowerment Bridge," had rapidly gained momentum. It was now operating in several countries, and the impact of its programs was evident in the success stories that flowed in from all directions. Nidhi, though busier than ever, felt a profound sense of purpose and fulfillment.

One morning, she received an invitation from the United Nations to participate in a panel discussion on global empowerment initiatives. The event was to be held in New York, and it was an honor she couldn't refuse. The prospect of sharing her work on such a prestigious platform filled her with both excitement and a sense of responsibility.

The panel discussion was held in the grand assembly hall of the United Nations headquarters. Nidhi found herself sitting alongside influential leaders, activists, and philanthropists. The session was focused on sustainable development goals, particularly on gender equality and education.

When it was her turn to speak, Nidhi took a deep breath, remembering Aisha's advice to stay grounded and authentic.

"Distinguished guests, it is an honor to be here today," she began. "Empowerment Bridge started as a vision to break the cycle of self-doubt and unlock the potential within individuals, especially those from marginalized communities. Our focus is not only on providing resources but also on fostering a mindset of resilience and self-belief."

She shared stories of women like Meera, whose lives had been transformed through education and mentorship. The audience was captivated, and Nidhi could feel the energy in the room shift as they connected with the real-world impact of her work.

"We believe that true empowerment comes from within," Nidhi continued. "By nurturing a positive mindset and providing the necessary support, we can create a ripple effect that changes communities and, ultimately, the world."

After the panel, Nidhi was approached by several attendees, including representatives from international organizations and government agencies. They expressed interest in collaborating with Empowerment Bridge to expand its reach and impact.

One particularly meaningful conversation was with Fatima, a young woman from Nigeria who had started a grassroots initiative to educate girls in rural areas. She was passionate, determined, and reminded Nidhi of herself.

"Your story resonates deeply with me," Fatima said. "I've faced many challenges, but your words have given me renewed hope and determination. I would love to collaborate and bring Empowerment Bridge to my community."

Nidhi felt a profound connection with Fatima. "I'm inspired by your work, Fatima. Let's join forces and make a difference together."

Back in her office, Nidhi and her team began strategizing on how to integrate Fatima's initiative with Empowerment Bridge. They developed a comprehensive plan that included training local educators, providing scholarships, and setting up community centers that would serve as hubs for learning and support.

The collaboration with Fatima's initiative was a huge success. It not only provided education and resources to girls in rural Nigeria but also empowered local women to become leaders and mentors in their communities. The program's success attracted attention from various media outlets, further amplifying their message.

As Empowerment Bridge continued to grow, Nidhi realized the importance of fostering a strong community among those they served. She organized an annual global summit, bringing together participants, mentors, and leaders from different countries to share their experiences and learn from each other.

The first Empowerment Bridge Global Summit was held in Mumbai. It was a vibrant, dynamic event filled with workshops, panel discussions, and networking opportunities. Nidhi opened the summit with a heartfelt speech, emphasizing the power of community and collaboration.

"Together, we are stronger," she said. "Each of you has a unique story and a valuable perspective. By coming together, we can learn, grow, and create even greater impact."

The summit was a resounding success. Participants left feeling inspired and motivated, armed with new knowledge and connections to continue their work. Nidhi herself felt rejuvenated, her vision for Empowerment Bridge reaffirmed and strengthened.

One evening, after the summit had concluded, Nidhi received a call from Aisha. They hadn't spoken in a while, and it was a welcome surprise.

"Nidhi, I've been following your progress," Aisha said, her voice filled with pride. "You've created something truly remarkable. How are you feeling about everything?"

Nidhi paused, reflecting on the journey so far. "I feel grateful, Aisha. It's been challenging but incredibly rewarding. I see the impact we're making, and it drives me to keep going."

Aisha's voice softened. "Remember to take care of yourself, too. Your well-being is just as important as your work."

Nidhi smiled, feeling the warmth of Aisha's care. "I will, Aisha. Thank you for always being there."

As the years passed, Nidhi continued to lead Empowerment Bridge with passion and dedication. The foundation's programs expanded to new regions, touching more lives and fostering a global community of empowered individuals.

Nidhi also took time for herself, nurturing her personal growth and maintaining her relationships with family and friends. She made sure to practice the self-care routines Aisha had taught her, ensuring she remained grounded and balanced amidst her busy schedule.

Her journey, once marked by self-doubt and insecurity, had transformed into one of empowerment and impact. Nidhi had discovered the true power within herself and had dedicated her life to helping others do the same.

One evening, as Nidhi sat on her balcony overlooking the city, she reflected on the incredible journey she had undertaken. From the depths of self-doubt to the heights of global recognition, she had not only transformed her own life but also the lives of countless others.

Her phone buzzed with a message from Meera, now a successful entrepreneur. "Thank you for believing in me, Nidhi. Your guidance changed my life."

Nidhi smiled, her heart swelling with pride and joy. She knew that the ripple effect of empowerment was continuing, reaching new heights with each passing day.

As she looked out at the city lights, Nidhi felt a deep sense of fulfillment. She had built bridges of empowerment and hope, and her journey was far from over. With unwavering determination and a heart full of compassion, she was ready to embrace the limitless possibilities of the future, knowing that the power to create positive change lay within her and within everyone she touched.

CHAPTER EIGHT

Global Impact

Nidhi's journey with Empowerment Bridge took on a new dimension as the foundation's reach expanded beyond borders. International partnerships and collaborations became a cornerstone of their efforts, amplifying their impact and spreading their message of empowerment to every corner of the globe.

One day, as Nidhi was reviewing potential projects with her team, she received an invitation from the United Nations to speak at a special summit on women's empowerment. It was an incredible opportunity to share the work of Empowerment Bridge on a global stage and to connect with leaders from around the world who were dedicated to advancing gender equality.

As she prepared for her speech, Nidhi felt a mix of excitement and nervousness. The stakes were high, but she knew that this was a chance to inspire change on a scale she had never imagined possible.

The day of the summit arrived, and Nidhi stood before a packed auditorium, her heart pounding with anticipation. As she spoke about the importance of empowering women and girls to reach their full potential, she felt a powerful sense of purpose wash over her.

Her words resonated with the audience, igniting a spark of inspiration in the hearts of all who listened. From government officials to grassroots activists, everyone in the room was united by a shared commitment to creating a more equitable and just world.

After her speech, Nidhi was approached by representatives from several countries who expressed interest in partnering with Empowerment Bridge to implement programs in their communities. It was a testament to the universal appeal of the foundation's mission and the growing recognition of the importance of mindset mastery in driving social change.

Excited by the possibilities, Nidhi and her team began exploring new avenues for collaboration, leveraging the foundation's expertise to address a wide range of issues, from education and healthcare to economic empowerment and environmental sustainability.

One of the most impactful partnerships was with a nonprofit organization in Southeast Asia that focused on providing vocational training and economic opportunities to marginalized women. Together, they developed a program that integrated mindset mastery techniques into their existing curriculum, empowering women to overcome barriers and pursue their entrepreneurial dreams.

The results were nothing short of transformative. Women who had once struggled to make ends meet now found themselves thriving as business owners and community leaders. Their success not only lifted themselves out of poverty but also inspired others to believe in the power of their own potential.

As Empowerment Bridge's global footprint continued to expand, Nidhi found herself traveling to new countries and cultures, each presenting its own unique opportunities and challenges. From remote villages in Africa to bustling metropolises in Latin America, she witnessed firsthand the transformative power of empowerment and resilience.

Everywhere she went, Nidhi was struck by the resilience and determination of the human spirit. Despite facing seemingly insurmountable obstacles, people from all walks of life were finding ways to overcome adversity and create a better future for themselves and their communities.

Back at the foundation's headquarters, Nidhi reflected on the incredible journey she had been on. From a corporate executive struggling with self-doubt to a global leader in empowerment, her path had been filled with twists and turns, challenges and triumphs. And yet, through it all, she had remained true to her vision of creating a world where everyone had the opportunity to thrive.

As she looked ahead to the future, Nidhi felt a renewed sense of purpose and determination. The journey was far from over, but she knew that with each new partnership and collaboration, Empowerment Bridge would continue to make a difference in the lives of people around the world.

And with that thought in mind, Nidhi rolled up her sleeves and got back to work, ready to take on whatever challenges lay ahead in the pursuit of a more just, equitable, and empowered world.

CHAPTER NINE

New Horizons

Nidhi's journey with Empowerment Bridge continued to evolve, branching out into new territories and exploring innovative ways to empower individuals and communities. Her foundation had become a beacon of hope and transformation, and its impact was felt far and wide.

One day, while reviewing a proposal for a new project in South America, Nidhi received an email from a prestigious university in Europe. They were inviting her to develop a curriculum based on the principles of mindset mastery and empowerment, aimed at both students and educators. The idea of shaping young minds and future leaders excited her, and she knew this was an opportunity she couldn't pass up.

In collaboration with the university, Nidhi began to craft a comprehensive course that incorporated the core tenets of Empowerment Bridge. The curriculum included modules on self-awareness, resilience, leadership, and community building. Nidhi drew from her own experiences and those of others she had mentored, creating a rich, engaging, and practical program.

As she worked on the curriculum, Nidhi realized the potential for this initiative to expand even further. She envisioned a global network of educational institutions adopting these principles, creating a new generation of empowered leaders ready to tackle the world's challenges with confidence and compassion.

The launch of the curriculum at the university was a resounding success. Students and educators alike were enthusiastic about the program, and the feedback was overwhelmingly positive. Encouraged by this success, Nidhi began reaching out to other universities and schools around the world, offering to share the curriculum and support its implementation.

Her efforts soon bore fruit. Institutions from different countries expressed interest, and Nidhi found herself traveling extensively to oversee the rollout of the program. Each new partnership brought unique challenges and rewards, and Nidhi cherished the opportunity to learn from diverse cultures and perspectives.

During one of her trips to Africa, Nidhi visited a rural school in Kenya that had recently adopted the curriculum. She was greeted with warm smiles and a vibrant energy that filled the air. The students were eager to share their experiences, and Nidhi listened intently as they spoke about how the program had inspired them to dream bigger and strive for excellence.

One student, a young girl named Amina, stood out to Nidhi. Amina spoke with a quiet confidence that belied her age, sharing her aspirations of becoming a doctor and returning to her village to improve healthcare.

"Nidhi, your program has given me the belief that I can achieve my dreams," Amina said, her eyes shining with determination. "I want to help my community and make a difference."

Nidhi felt a surge of pride and hope. "Amina, you have the power within you to achieve anything you set your mind to. Keep believing in yourself, and never let go of your dreams."

Back at the foundation's headquarters, Nidhi and her team were busy preparing for the annual Empowerment Bridge Global Summit. This year, the summit was to be held in Nairobi, and it promised to be the largest and most impactful gathering yet.

The theme of the summit was "New Horizons," reflecting the foundation's expanding reach and the boundless potential of its mission. Participants from all over the world were invited to share their stories, exchange ideas, and forge new partnerships.

The opening ceremony was a grand affair, with a diverse audience of leaders, educators, and changemakers. Nidhi stood at the podium, feeling a profound sense of gratitude and purpose.

"Welcome to the Empowerment Bridge Global Summit," she began.

"Today, we celebrate the incredible journeys of transformation and empowerment that each of you represents. Together, we are building a brighter future, one filled with hope, resilience, and limitless possibilities."

The summit was a whirlwind of activity, with workshops, panels, and networking sessions that buzzed with energy and enthusiasm. Nidhi was particularly moved by a session where young leaders from different continents shared their innovative projects and visions for the future. Their passion and creativity were infectious, and Nidhi felt inspired by their commitment to making a difference.

As the summit drew to a close, Nidhi took a moment to reflect on the incredible progress made since the inception of Empowerment Bridge. The foundation had grown beyond her wildest dreams, and its impact was a testament to the power of community and the human spirit.

One evening, while watching the sunset over Nairobi, Nidhi received a message from Aisha. "Congratulations on the summit, Nidhi. You've built something truly extraordinary. How are you feeling?"

Nidhi smiled, her heart full. "Thank you, Aisha. I'm feeling incredibly grateful and inspired. The journey has been challenging, but seeing the impact we've made is worth every effort."

Aisha's reply was warm and encouraging. "Your journey is a testament to what's possible when we believe in ourselves and each other. Keep shining, Nidhi. The world needs more of your light."

With the summit's success and the continued expansion of the curriculum, Nidhi's vision for Empowerment Bridge only grew stronger. She knew that there were still many more horizons to explore, many more lives to touch. As she looked out at the vast landscape before her, she felt a deep sense of purpose and an unwavering commitment to her mission.

The journey ahead was filled with possibilities, and Nidhi was ready to embrace each new challenge with the same determination and resilience that had brought her this far. She had discovered the limitless power within herself, and she was dedicated to helping others do the same, creating a world where everyone could reach their full potential and build a future filled with hope, empowerment, and endless horizons.

CHAPTER TEN

Legacy of Empowerment

The years following the summit in Nairobi saw Empowerment Bridge reach unprecedented heights. Nidhi's vision continued to expand, influencing not just individual lives but entire communities and systems. The educational curriculum she had developed was now part of schools and universities across the globe, fostering a generation of empowered, self-aware, and resilient individuals.

Nidhi's work began attracting attention from global leaders and organizations. She was invited to speak at various international forums, sharing her insights and experiences on mindset mastery and empowerment. Her message resonated deeply, and she found herself becoming a thought leader in the realm of personal development and social change.

One day, while preparing for a keynote speech at a major global conference, Nidhi received a call from Meera, now a successful entrepreneur and a mentor within Empowerment Bridge.

"Nidhi, I have exciting news," Meera said, her voice brimming with enthusiasm. "I've been selected to receive the Global Innovators Award for my work in sustainable business practices!"

Nidhi felt a surge of pride and joy. "Meera, that's incredible! Your hard work and dedication have truly paid off. I'm so proud of you."

Meera's journey had come full circle, and she was now inspiring others just as Nidhi had inspired her. It was a testament to the ripple effect of empowerment that Nidhi had always believed in.

The conference where Nidhi was to speak was held in Geneva, and it brought together leaders from various fields to discuss solutions to the world's most pressing challenges. Nidhi's session focused on the role of mindset and community in driving sustainable development and social change.

Standing on stage, Nidhi felt a familiar sense of purpose and excitement.

"Good morning, everyone," she began. "Today, I want to talk about the profound impact that a shift in mindset can have on individuals, communities, and the world at large."

She shared the story of Empowerment Bridge, highlighting the transformative journeys of people like Meera and Amina. Her words resonated with the audience, many of whom approached her afterward, eager to learn more and collaborate.

Among those who reached out was a representative from the World Bank, who expressed interest in partnering with Empowerment Bridge to integrate mindset training into economic development programs. Nidhi was thrilled at the prospect of scaling the foundation's impact even further.

Back at the headquarters, Nidhi and her team worked tirelessly to develop a proposal for the World Bank partnership. They crafted a comprehensive plan that included workshops, training sessions, and community engagement initiatives designed to foster a mindset of resilience and empowerment.

The partnership was approved, and soon, Empowerment Bridge was working in collaboration with the World Bank to implement programs in developing countries. The initiative was a game-changer, helping communities build not only economic stability but also a strong foundation of self-belief and empowerment.

One evening, as Nidhi was reflecting on the incredible journey of Empowerment Bridge, she received a video call from Fatima. The screen lit up with Fatima's bright smile, and Nidhi could see the bustling activity of a community center in the background.

"Nidhi, I wanted to show you something," Fatima said, turning the camera to reveal a group of young girls eagerly working on a science project. "This is one of the new community centers we've established with your support. These girls are full of dreams and determination, and it's all because of the opportunities we've been able to provide."

Nidhi felt tears of joy well up in her eyes. "Fatima, this is beautiful. Seeing the impact of our work firsthand is the greatest reward. Thank you for sharing this with me."

As Empowerment Bridge continued to flourish, Nidhi found herself thinking about the future. She knew that the foundation's work would need to evolve and adapt to new challenges and opportunities. With this in mind, she began planning for a leadership transition, ensuring that Empowerment Bridge would continue to thrive even beyond her direct involvement.

She identified potential successors within her team, mentoring and guiding them to take on more significant roles. Meera and Fatima were among those she considered, both having demonstrated exceptional leadership and a deep commitment to the foundation's mission.

In a special board meeting, Nidhi announced her intention to step back from her day-to-day role, transitioning to an advisory position. She introduced Meera and Fatima as the new co-leaders of Empowerment Bridge, confident in their ability to carry the torch forward.

"It has been an honor and a privilege to lead Empowerment Bridge," Nidhi said, addressing the board and her team. "I am incredibly proud of what we have achieved together, and I am confident that under Meera and Fatima's leadership, the foundation will continue to grow and create lasting impact."

The room erupted in applause, and Nidhi felt a deep sense of fulfillment. She knew that Empowerment Bridge was in good hands and that its legacy of empowerment would endure.

As she transitioned into her new advisory role, Nidhi took some time to reflect on her journey. From a corporate executive grappling with self-doubt to a global leader in empowerment, her path had been transformative and deeply rewarding.

One afternoon, she sat on her balcony, watching the sunset. Her phone buzzed with a message from Aisha.

"Congratulations on the transition, Nidhi. You've built a lasting legacy. How do you feel?"

Nidhi smiled, her heart full of gratitude. "Thank you, Aisha. I feel fulfilled and excited for the future. The journey has been incredible, and I'm looking forward to seeing where it leads next."

Aisha's response was warm and encouraging. "You've done extraordinary work, Nidhi. Remember, the ripple effect of empowerment will continue to grow, thanks to the foundation you've built. Enjoy this new chapter."

As Nidhi looked out at the horizon, she felt a profound sense of peace and accomplishment. Her journey had not only transformed her own life but also the lives of countless others. The power of empowerment, she realized, was limitless, and its impact would continue to unfold in ways she could only imagine.

With a heart full of hope and a mind open to new possibilities, Nidhi embraced the next chapter of her life, knowing that the legacy of Empowerment Bridge would continue to inspire and uplift generations to come.

CHAPTER ELEVEN

Passing the Torch

As the years passed, Empowerment Bridge continued to thrive under the leadership of Meera and Fatima. The foundation's impact grew exponentially, reaching new communities and transforming countless lives. Nidhi remained closely involved as an advisor, offering guidance and support whenever needed.

One day, as Nidhi was reviewing a progress report from Empowerment Bridge, she received an unexpected visit from Aisha. It had been years since they had seen each other in person, and Nidhi was delighted by the surprise.

"Aisha, it's so wonderful to see you," Nidhi exclaimed, embracing her friend warmly. "To what do I owe this unexpected visit?"

Aisha smiled, her eyes sparkling with warmth. "I wanted to congratulate you on the incredible work you've done with Empowerment Bridge. Your vision and dedication have truly made a difference in the world."

Nidhi felt a swell of emotion as she looked at Aisha. "Thank you, Aisha. None of this would have been possible without your guidance and support. You helped me find the strength and courage to embark on this journey."

As they sat together in Nidhi's office, Aisha shared news of a new project she was working on—a global initiative focused on mental health and well-being. She explained how the program aimed to destigmatize mental health issues and provide support to individuals struggling with anxiety, depression, and other challenges.

Nidhi was deeply inspired by Aisha's vision. "Mental health is such an important issue, and it's often overlooked or misunderstood. Your initiative could have a profound impact on so many lives."

Aisha nodded, her expression serious yet determined. "That's why I wanted to talk to you, Nidhi. I believe that Empowerment Bridge and my new initiative share a common goal—to empower individuals to overcome their inner struggles and live fulfilling lives."

Nidhi's heart skipped a beat as she realized what Aisha was suggesting. "Are you proposing a partnership between Empowerment Bridge and your new initiative?"

Aisha smiled, her eyes shining with excitement. "Exactly. I believe that together, we can create a comprehensive support system that addresses both the external challenges people face and the internal obstacles to their well-being."

Over the following weeks, Nidhi and Aisha worked closely together to develop a plan for the partnership. They identified areas of overlap between Empowerment Bridge's programs and Aisha's mental health initiative, exploring how they could complement each other and provide holistic support to individuals in need.

One of the key components of the partnership was a series of workshops and support groups focused on mental health and emotional well-being. These sessions would integrate mindfulness practices, cognitive-behavioral techniques, and peer support to help participants develop resilience and coping skills.

Nidhi was excited by the possibilities of the partnership. "Aisha, this has the potential to be truly transformative. By addressing both the external and internal factors that impact people's lives, we can create a more holistic approach to empowerment and well-being."

Aisha nodded in agreement. "I couldn't agree more, Nidhi. Together, we can break down the barriers that prevent people from living their best lives and create a world where everyone has the opportunity to thrive."

The launch of the partnership between Empowerment Bridge and Aisha's mental health initiative was met with widespread enthusiasm. Participants from all walks of life flocked to the workshops and support groups, eager to learn and grow together.

Nidhi and Aisha were invited to speak at conferences and events around the world, sharing their insights and experiences with audiences eager to learn from their expertise. Their partnership became a beacon of hope and inspiration, demonstrating the power of collaboration in creating positive change.

As they traveled together, Nidhi and Aisha reflected on their journey and the impact they had made. From their humble beginnings to their current roles as leaders in the fields of empowerment and mental health, they had come a long way. And yet, they knew that their work was far from over.

One evening, as they sat together overlooking the city lights, Nidhi turned to Aisha with a smile. "Thank you, Aisha. For everything."

Aisha returned the smile, her eyes reflecting the warmth of their shared journey. "No, Nidhi. Thank you. For your courage, your vision, and your unwavering commitment to making the world a better place."

As they sat in companionable silence, watching the stars twinkle overhead, Nidhi felt a deep sense of gratitude wash over her. She knew that their partnership would continue to touch lives and inspire change for years to come, leaving a legacy of empowerment and well-being that would endure for generations. And she couldn't wait to see what the future held.

CHAPTER TWELVE

The Legacy Continues

Years passed, and the partnership between Empowerment Bridge and Aisha's mental health initiative flourished. Together, they touched the lives of countless individuals, offering support, guidance, and hope to those in need. Nidhi and Aisha continued to work tirelessly, driven by their shared vision of a world where everyone could thrive.

One day, as Nidhi sat in her office reflecting on the journey that had brought her to this point, she received a package in the mail. It was a book—a collection of stories from people whose lives had been transformed by Empowerment Bridge and Aisha's mental health initiative.

As she flipped through the pages, Nidhi was moved by the words of gratitude and inspiration. Each story was a testament to the power of empowerment and resilience, and to the impact that one person—or two, in Nidhi and Aisha's case—could have on the world.

At a special event to launch the book, Nidhi and Aisha stood together on stage, surrounded by friends, colleagues, and supporters. As they addressed the audience, their voices filled with emotion, they reflected on the incredible journey they had shared.

"It's been an honor and a privilege to work alongside Nidhi," Aisha said, her eyes shining with pride. "Together, we've seen the transformative power of empowerment and resilience, and we've witnessed the incredible strength of the human spirit."

Nidhi nodded in agreement, her heart overflowing with gratitude. "And it's been a privilege to work alongside Aisha," she said. "Her wisdom, compassion, and unwavering belief in the potential of every individual have been a constant source of inspiration."

As the event came to a close, Nidhi and Aisha stepped off the stage and into the embrace of their friends and colleagues. They knew that their work was far from over, but they also knew that they had laid a strong foundation for the future.

As they looked out at the faces of those gathered around them, Nidhi and Aisha felt a profound sense of gratitude and fulfillment. They knew that the legacy of Empowerment Bridge and Aisha's mental health initiative would continue to inspire and uplift generations to come.

And as they walked hand in hand into the sunset, they knew that their journey was far from over. With hearts full of hope and minds open to new possibilities, they embraced the next chapter of their lives, knowing that the legacy they had built would continue to shine brightly for years to come.

And so, as the sun dipped below the horizon, casting a warm glow over the world, Nidhi and Aisha looked ahead to the future, ready to continue their journey of empowerment, resilience, and hope. And as they took their first steps into the unknown, they knew that the best was yet to come.

The End.

End Note

As we close the pages of this story, we are reminded of the profound impact that each of us can have on the world. Through courage, compassion, and unwavering determination, Nidhi and Aisha embarked on a journey of empowerment and resilience, touching the lives of countless individuals along the way.

Their story serves as a reminder that no dream is too big, no obstacle too daunting, and no journey too challenging when we believe in ourselves and each other. As we navigate the ups and downs of life, may we draw inspiration from Nidhi and Aisha's example, and may we always strive to create a world where everyone has the opportunity to thrive.

Let their legacy be a beacon of hope and possibility, guiding us forward with courage and conviction. And may we never forget the power of empowerment, resilience, and the human spirit to transform lives and shape the world for the better.

With gratitude and optimism,
Nidhi Dohare

www.ingramcontent.com/pod-product-compliance
Lightning Source LLC
LaVergne TN
LVHW021144160826
845679LV00023B/2041

* 9 7 9 8 8 9 4 4 6 8 3 0 3 *